Weather Activity Book

Author	Charlene Stout
Editor	Kathy Rogers
Page Design	Linda Milliken
Artist	Barb Lorseyedi
Cover Design	Imaginings

METRIC CONVERSION CHART

Refer to this chart when metric conversions are not found within the activity.

¼ tsp	=	1 ml	350° F	=	180° C
½ tsp	=	2 ml	375° F	=	190° C
1 tsp	=	5 ml	400° F	=	200° C
1 Tbsp	=	15 ml	425° F	=	216° C
¼ cup	=	60 ml	1 inch	=	2.54 cm
⅓ cup	=	80 ml	1 foot	=	30 cm
½ cup	=	125 ml	1 yard	=	91 cm
1 cup	=	250 ml	1 mile	=	1.6 km
1 oz.	=	28 g			
1 lb.	=	.45 kg			

www.edupressinc.com
ISBN 1-56472-123-X
Printed in USA

Table of Contents

Literature List

• ***Deadly Storms in Action***
by Marianne Borgardt;
Intervisual Books 1991. (3-6)
A pop-up action book about tornadoes, hurricanes, lightning storms, blizzards, floods, and the greenhouse effect.

• ***What Makes It Rain? The Story of a Raindrop***
by Keith Brandt;
Troll 1982. (1-3)
The story of the water cycle told as a journey taken by every drop of water that falls to Earth.

• ***It's Raining Cats and Dogs***
by Franklyn Branley;
Houghton 1987. (3-6)
Strange weather happenings are mixed with scientific accounts of the weather.

• ***What Will the Weather Be?***
by Lynda DeWitt;
Harper 1991. ((K-3)
An illustrated introduction to weather forecasting.

• ***McBroom and the Big Wind***
by Sid Fleischman;
Grosset 1967. (3-6)
A tall tale that humorously shows effects of wind on people, plants, and animals.

• ***Weather Forecasting***
by Gail Gibbons;
Macmillan 1987. (K-3)
Touring a weather station during the four seasons.

• ***Weatherwise; Learning about Weather***
by Jonathan Kahl;
Lerner 1992. (4-6)
Topics covered include atmosphere, winds, storms, and forecasting.

• ***Our Global Greenhouse***
by April Koral;
Watts 1989. (4-6)
A book about problems of, issues in, and possible solutions to the greenhouse effect.

• ***Here Comes Jack Frost***
by Sharon Peters;
Troll 1981. (K-2)
This easy reader paints the fairy tale of Jack Frost with beautifully swirling illustrations.

• ***The Weather***
by Roy Richardson;
Watts 1993. (1-2)
For very young children, this introductory account explains atmosphere, kinds of weather, and weather forecasting.

• ***Frost: Causes and Effects***
by Philip Steele;
Watts 1991.(3-6)
A brief overview with full-color photos of how frost forms and what it does.

• ***Storm in the Night***
by Mary Stolz;
Harper Trophy 1988. (3-6)
During a thunderstorm, Grandfather spins his childhood storm stories with sights, sounds, smells, and the emotions of fear.

• ***Snow, Ice and Cold***
by Bernard Stonehouse;
Macmillan 1993. (5-7)
This work tells about how individuals and cultures have adjusted to severe cold climates.

• ***Now I Know About Clouds***
by Roy Wandelmaier;
Troll 1985. (K-3)
In simple and visual terms, this book names, describes, and defines the types of clouds.

Glossary

anemometer—an instrument that measures the wind's speed.

atmosphere—the layers of gases (air) that surrounds the earth, mostly nitrogen and oxygen.

aurora borealis—a spectacular curtain-like display of lights in the sky.

barometer—an instrument that measures air pressure in millibars or millimeters.

Celsius scale—the centigrade temperature scale divided into 100 degree markings. Water boils at 10°C. and freezes at 0°C.

cloud—a white or gray mass of millions of tiny droplets of water or ice crystals floating together in the sky.

condensation—the process of vapor changing into a liquid.

Coriolis effect—the twisting of air currents caused by the rotation of the Earth.

doldrums—the area surrounding the equator where there is little or no wind.

drought—a long period of time with little or no rainfall.

el nino—a warming of ocean water that wreaks havoc on the weather systems.

evaporation—the process of a solid or liquid changing into a vapor.

front—the line of changing weather between highs and lows.

frost—tiny ice crystals that form on glass when the air is below freezing.

high—the clockwise winds in the Northern Hemisphere; the counterclockwise in the Southern Hemisphere.

humidity—the amount of water vapor present in the air.

lightning—a sudden bright flash of light seen in the sky during a thunderstorm.

low—the winds that rotate counterclockwise in the Northern Hemisphere, clockwise in the Southern Hemisphere.

meteorologist—the official name of a weather expert.

precipitation—the falling of water from clouds in the form of rain, sleet, hail, or snow.

prism—a solid three-sided transparent object that can break a ray of sunlight into rainbow colors.

rain gauge—an instrument that measures the amount of rainfall in inches or millimeters.

smog—a mix of smoke and fog in the air.

spectrum—the colors within a band of white light.

temperature—heat in the air.

thermometer—an instrument that measures the temperature of the air.

water cycle—water in the Earth's atmosphere moving and changing in a circle of rising vapor (evaporation), droplets collecting together in clouds (condensation), and falling as liquid or ice (precipitation).

Elements of Weather

Information

The four main elements that make up weather are **temperature, wind, moisture, and air pressure.**

Project

Create a poster for each element and display accordion-style.

Materials

- Four poster boards
- Weather resource books
- Construction paper
- Water paints and brushes
- Scissors
- Glue
- Tape

Directions

1. Divide class into four small groups.
2. Direct each group to choose one element, brainstorm, and do research.
3. Create a collage for each element.
4. Tape the element collages together accordion-style for display.

Temperature

Temperature affects the weather more than anything else. Our sun hurls huge amounts of energy into space. Some reaches Earth. We call that sunshine. Some is reflected back into space.

A thick layer of air that surrounds the Earth (atmosphere) traps the sunshine just like a greenhouse does. Plants in the Earth's greenhouse absorb some of the energy, changing it into heat.

Wind

Because heat is trapped in our Earthly greenhouse, we depend on winds to carry the excess stored-up heat from the equator in a circular pattern, upward to the icy polar regions. Here the cooler, heavier air sinks downward under the warmer air that is rising. The movement of the warm air going up and the cooler air pushing in under makes a wind.

Air Pressure

Air constantly presses down on us. At times the air rises like towering transparent mountains, peaking high in the air. Weather forecasters call these *high-pressure* areas. They love predicting the fair weather and sunny skies that follow.

Between the mountains of high pressure air, there are whirling valleys of *low-pressure* air. Here hot wet air from one invisible mountain mixes with cold, dry air from another to bring cloudy or stormy weather.

Moisture

Moisture is tiny drops of water that rise up (evaporate) from the ground and from bodies of water. We don't really see the water evaporate, but we do see puddles disappear and wet clothes become dry on the clothesline.

Moisture rises and clings to tiny dust pieces until it forms droplets. These fall to earth as rain, sleet, or snow and starts the trip all over again—evaporating, forming drops, falling, puddling, evaporating, forming drops, falling, puddling…

Seasonal Weather

Information

The four seasons bring dramatic changes in temperature, weather, and the length of daylight. Some regions of the world do not have all four seasons. In the tropics temperatures change little. Instead, there is a wet and a dry season. The polar regions have a light and a dark season, with sunshine and warm temperatures almost all the time in summer and almost never in the winter.

In Alaska, temperatures can range from -80°F (-17°C) in winter to as high as 100°F (38°C) in summer. For this reason Alaska is a good example of how weather affects people, plants, animals, and the Earth. With 20 hours of sunshine in the summer, fruits and vegetables grow rapidly. Weather changes there have a striking effect on people's moods, clothing, and activities. The extreme weather makes road-building difficult and costly. Native animals change coloring to survive.

Project

Create four books, one about each season, showing the effects that weather has on people, plants, animals, and the world in general.

Materials

- White construction paper
- Stapler
- Crayons, colored pens, or pencils

Directions

1. Divide class into four groups, one for each season.
2. Assign research on the season's affect upon people, plants, animals, and the Earth.
3. Fold and staple paper into book form.
4. Share books with the class and put on display.

Effects of Weather

Information

Weather is what is happening in the air around us. It changes constantly. It affects all of us. Weather makes our skin feel hot and sweaty or cold and clammy. A sudden shower can soak us to the skin.

We cannot change the weather but we can adjust ourselves to it—light cotton and linen clothing in summer, waterproof rainwear for showery days, woolen clothing and warm boots for snowy blizzards, sun block for scorching hot days.

Project

Design all-weather clothing using the best materials to protect stick puppets from the elements of extreme weather.

Directions

1. To make a stick puppet, draw the shape of a person on cardboard and cut out. Use markers or crayons to decorate. Glue to craft stick.
2. Choose one extreme element of weather and design an outfit to protect each puppet.
3. Present a puppet show in which each puppet describes their clothing and how it is designed to protect them from the element of weather they represent.

Materials

- Cardboard
- Crayons or markers
- Scissors
- Craft sticks
- Glue
- Fabric and soft plastic squares

Weather Moods

Information

With weather changes come changes in our moods. Bright sunshine makes our day cheerful. Fog casts a gloomy mood. Snow delights the young-at-heart with sledding, skating, or skiing. That same snow exhausts the elderly snow-shoveler and frustrates the weary traveler. Being aware of the effect weather has on our moods can help us better understand and control our reactions to things that go on around us.

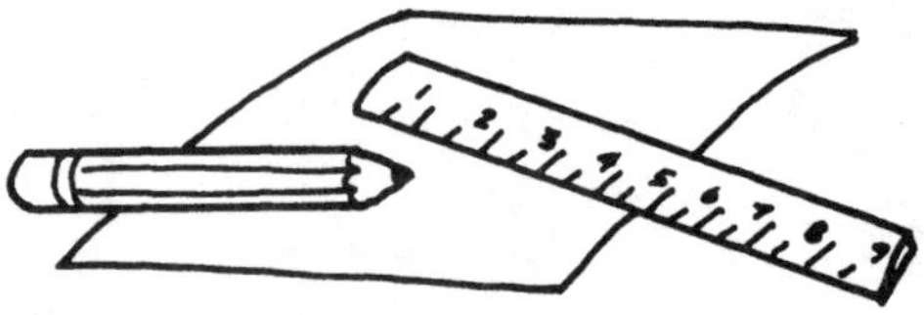

Project

Make a mood wheel to reflect emotions felt during different types of weather.

Materials

- Cardboard
- Scissors
- Metal brad
- Marking pens
- Ruler

Directions

1. Cut an 8-inch (20-cm) circle from lightweight cardboard.
2. Use the marking pen to divide the circle into eight pie-shaped sections.
3. Cut an arrow from cardboard. Attach it with a metal brad to the center of the cardboard circle.
4. Brainstorm a list of different moods, then choose eight to write on the mood wheel.
5. Keep the mood wheel on each desktop. Ask children to indicate their mood each day. Take a few moments to discuss the effect the day's weather might have on how they are feeling.

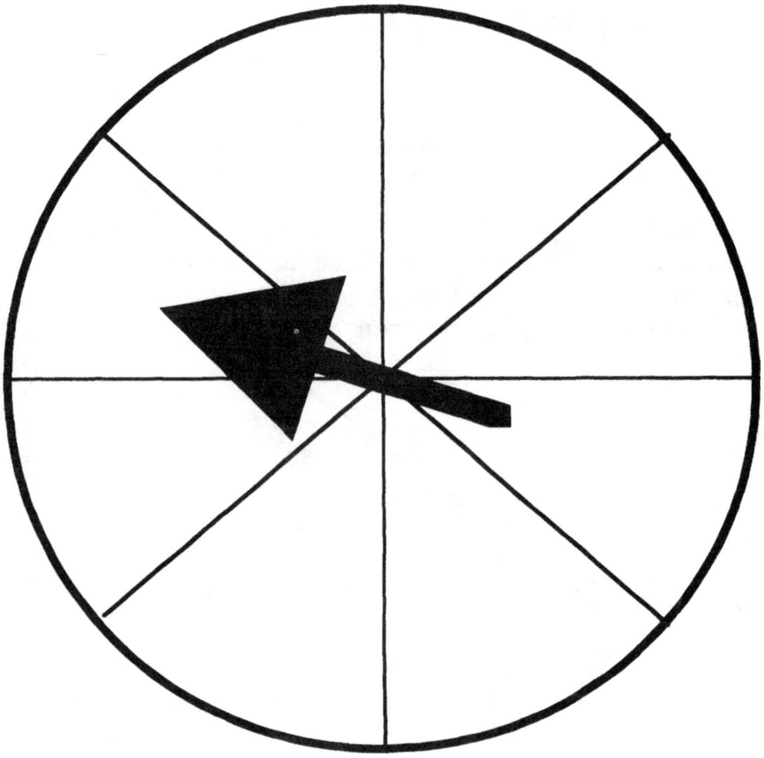

Prevailing Winds

Information

Wind is air moving across the Earth's surface. It is caused by the uneven heating of the Earth's atmosphere. Winds are named according to the direction **from** which they are blowing. In a process called *circulation*, layers of air are warmed by the sun, the warm air rising and colder air rushing in underneath. This produces six large belts of *prevailing winds* around the world.

There are no winds in the *doldrums* near the *equator* because there the warm air simply rises. Some of the air that rises from the equator returns to the Earth's surface at about 30° north and south latitudes. The downward-moving air produces no wind in the *horse latitudes*, named because so many horses died on ships stalled there by the lack of wind. The belts that lie between the equator and the horse latitudes were named *trade winds* by sailors of early sailing trading ships who depended on them.

Project

Create a classroom map showing the wind belts and prevailing winds of the world.

Materials

- Butcher paper
- Pencil
- Crayons or tempera paint and brushes
- Black pen for labels

Directions

1. Use crayons or tempera paint and brushes to create a simple map containing major landforms and oceans on a large piece of butcher paper.
2. Add the prevailing winds as arrows, showing the direction from which they are blowing.
3. Label the poles and each of the prevailing winds by name.

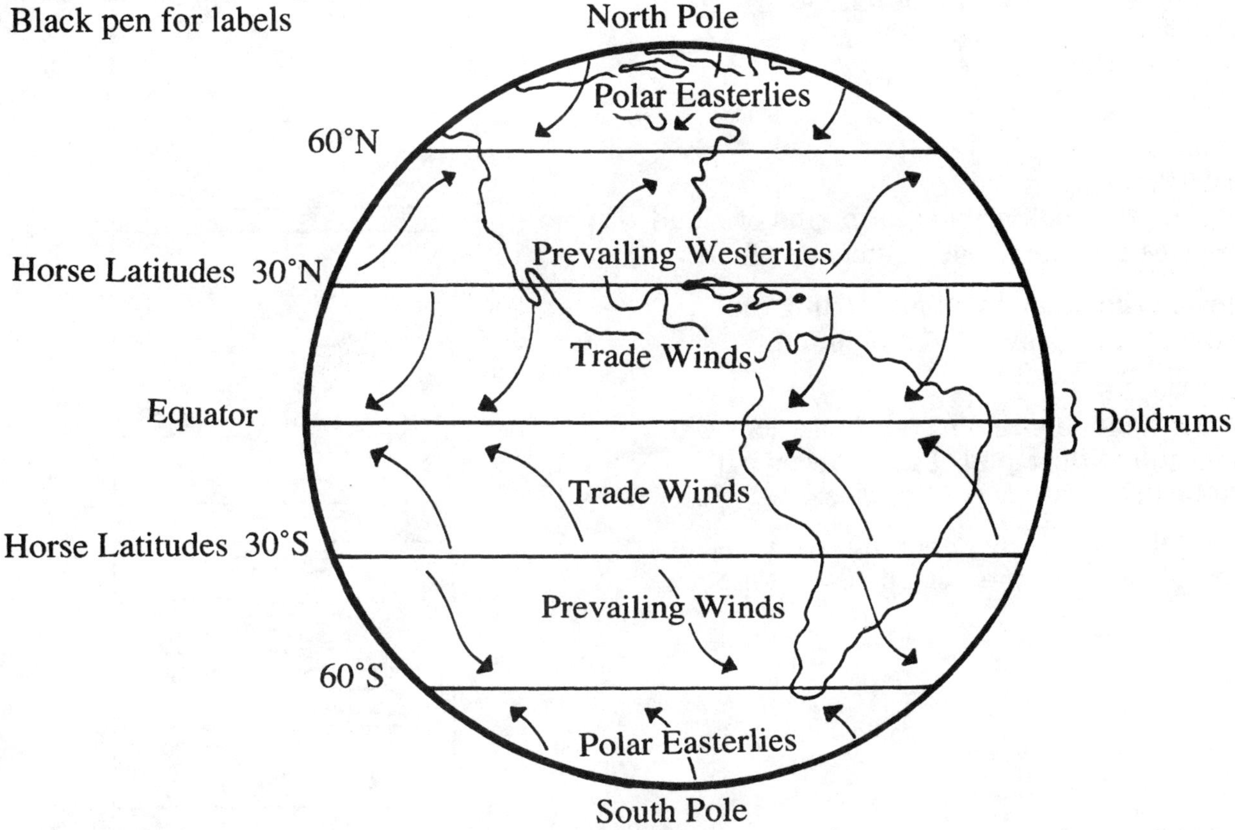

Clouds

Information

Forecasters, farmers, pilots, golfers, lifeguards, and picnickers all watch the clouds. They know that clouds can bring fair or foul weather, from fair breezes and warm air to rain, sleet, hail, and snow.

There are four kinds of clouds. Each looks different and is responsible for generating changing weather conditions. Two kinds of fair weather clouds are *cirrus* and *cumulus* clouds. The foul weather clouds are the *stratus* and *nimbus* clouds.

Project

Create a wall hanging that shows the different cloud formations. Complete a chart using clouds to predict weather conditions.

Materials

- Four half-sheets light blue construction paper
- Cloud Watcher's Chart, following
- Cotton balls
- White or blue yarn
- Scissors
- Glue
- Crayons

Directions

1. Share the information about each kind of cloud as described on the Cloud Watcher's Chart.
2. Recreate each cloud by manipulating the cotton balls and gluing them on blue construction paper.
3. Label each cloud with its correct name. Color a scene below the clouds that shows what might be happening weather-wise.
3. Connect the clouds by punching two holes at the top of each paper and tying them together with yarn.

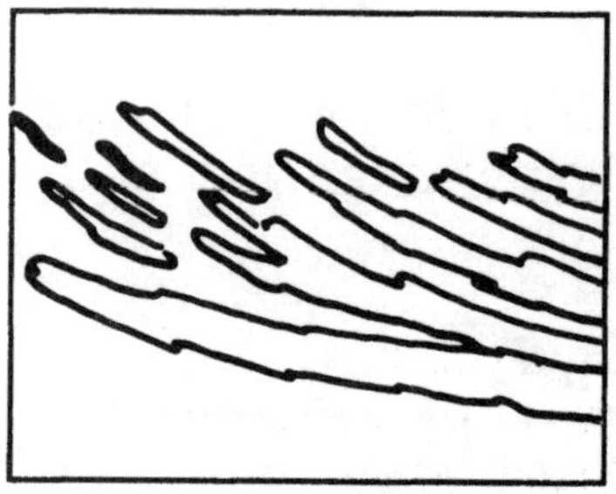

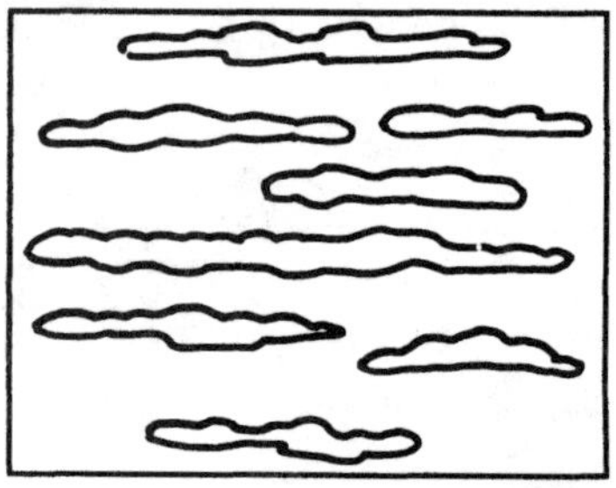

Cloud Watcher's Chart

Read about the different kinds of clouds. Beginning on Monday, look at the clouds in the sky. Record the kind you see on the chart next to the correct day. Predict the day's weather based on what you know about clouds. How accurate were you?

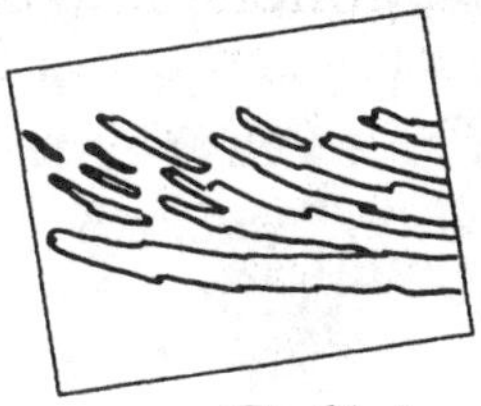

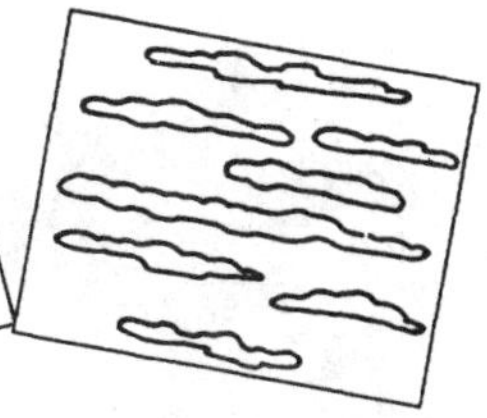

Cirrus

Cirrus, meaning "light and curly," are clouds found high in the sky in big open spaces. They are like thin, wispy, curls of white hair.

Cirrus clouds are so high the water is frozen into ice crystals. These clouds often come ahead of a storm.

Cumulus

Cumulus, meaning "heap or pile," are clouds that look like giant balls of cotton heaped up on a flat plate. They are always moving and swelling. On sunny days their white tops glisten in the sunlight. But they can quickly turn into cumulo-nimbus clouds.

Stratus

Stratus, meaning "spread out" are flat clouds that look like a dirty gray sheet blocking out the blue sky. Most often seen in the morning, they are like layers of heavy fog lifted up only slightly from earth. They often bring misty rain.

Nimbus

Nimbus, meaning "rainstorm," are menacing, black storm clouds that reach miles up into the sky, bringing wind, rain, hail, thunder, and lightning.

DAY	CLOUD TYPE	PREDICTION
MONDAY		
TUESDAY		
WEDNESDAY		
THURSDAY		
FRIDAY		
MONDAY		
TUESDAY		
WEDNESDAY		
THURSDAY		
FRIDAY		

Beaufort Wind Scale

Information

The Beaufort Wind Scale is a system for measuring wind speeds using a charted series of numbers from 0 to 17. The scale is used to help estimate and chart wind speeds both on land and sea. It was devised in 1805 by an admiral in the British navy named Sir Francis Beaufort.

The chart has been changed over the years. The chart used in 1874 simply defined the numbers according to the different winds' effect on sailing ships. For example, #12 stood for, "That which no canvas could withstand." Today, the Beaufort Scale assigns a Beaufort number and a symbol. It also names the wind with a descriptive word, gives wind speeds in miles-per-hour measured 10 meters (about 33 feet) above the ground, and lists the visible effects of the wind.

Project

Create a large Beaufort Wind Scale, adding pictures to illustrate the effect of each wind category.

Materials

- Butcher paper
- Black marking pens
- Ruler
- Pencil
- Scissors
- Colored pens or pencils
- Tape

Directions

1. Enlarge the grid for the Beaufort Wind Scale on butcher paper, omitting words, numbers, and symbols. Add a sixth column for students' pictures.
2. Cut the chart into 12 sections.
3. Divide the class into 12 small groups. Give each group one section to complete with both information and an illustration.
4. Reassemble the Wind Scale with tape.
5. Allow each group to explain their section to the class. Put on display.

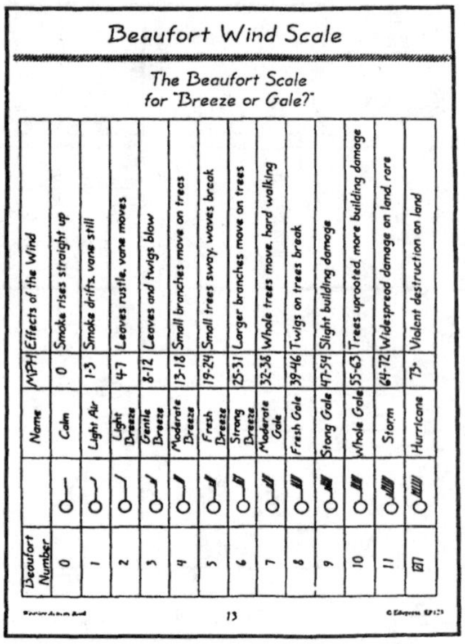

Beaufort Wind Scale

The Beaufort Scale for "Breeze or Gale?"

Beaufort Number		Name	MPH	Effects of the Wind
0		Calm	0	Smoke rises straight up
1		Light Air	1-3	Smoke drifts, vane still
2		Light Breeze	4-7	Leaves rustle, vane moves
3		Gentle Breeze	8-12	Leaves and twigs blow
4		Moderate Breeze	13-18	Small branches move on trees
5		Fresh Breeze	19-24	Small trees sway, waves break
6		Strong Breeze	25-31	Larger branches move on trees
7		Moderate Gale	32-38	Whole trees move, hard walking
8		Fresh Gale	39-46	Twigs on trees break
9		Stong Gale	47-54	Slight building damage
10		Whole Gale	55-63	Trees uprooted, more building damage
11		Storm	64-72	Widespread damage on land, rare
12		Hurricane	73+	Violent destruction on land

13

Beaufort Wind Scale

The Beaufort Scale for "Breeze or Gale?"

Beaufort Number	Name	MPH	Effects of the Wind
0	Calm	0	Smoke rises straight up
1	Light Air	1-3	Smoke drifts, vane still
2	Light Breeze	4-7	Leaves rustle, vane moves
3	Gentle Breeze	8-12	Leaves and twigs blow
4	Moderate Breeze	13-18	Small branches move on trees
5	Fresh Breeze	19-24	Small trees sway, waves break
6	Strong Breeze	25-31	Larger branches move on trees
7	Moderate Gale	32-38	Whole trees move, hard walking
8	Fresh Gale	39-46	Twigs on trees break
9	Strong Gale	47-54	Slight building damage
10	Whole Gale	55-63	Trees uprooted, more building damage
11	Storm	64-72	Widespread damage on land, rare
12 - 17	Hurricane	73+	Violent destruction on land

Hurricanes

Information

Hurricanes are huge, spiraling storms that are formed over the waters of the Atlantic Ocean. Most of them stay there. Hurricanes bring howling winds and heavy rains. The moist tropical air near the equator is heated by the sun and a gigantic upward spiral begins to grow. The calm air inside the spiral, known as the "eye" of the storm, can be more than 15 miles (24 km) across. Around the eye, circling winds, rain, and clouds can extend over 600 miles (966 km). Hurricane winds have been clocked at over 250 miles (402 km) per hour!

The biggest threat from a hurricane is the "storm surge," a huge wall of water as much as 25 feet (7.62 m) high that is pushed ahead of the hurricane by winds. When it reaches land, it comes crashing down, flooding the communities in low coastal areas. Hurricane winds and floods damage property, uproot large trees, bring down power lines, and destroy lives.

Project

Create windstorms in miniature to experience the different forces and strengths of wind.

Directions

1. Set up a large floor or table-top town, using milk cartons for houses and buildings, cut-outs for people, animals, and cars. Anchor with clay or tape.
2. Have children sit near enough to observe the effects of the winds and experience its force at different levels. Discuss the experiments that follow, relating each wind to the Beaufort Wind Scale and suggesting other effects.
3. Experiment with the various speeds on the blow dryer and observe the effects of concentrated winds on the town.
4. Experiment with a small hand vacuum and observe the suction effect of tornadoes on the town. Let students feel the suction on their hands.
5. Experiment with broader fan-created winds. Contrast damage from concentrated winds, suction winds, and wide area winds.
6. Draw conclusions and relate to thunderstorms, tornadoes, and hurricanes.

Materials

- Individual-sized milk cartons
- Construction paper
- Crayons
- Scissors
- Clay or tape
- Hand-held blow dryer
- Large powerful fan
- Small hand vacuum

Tornadoes

Information

No matter what you call them—funnel, twister, cyclone, or tornado—these fierce storms wreak havoc on lives in just a few minutes' time. Scientists watch for cold dry air moving in from the north, and warm moist air from the south. Powerful thunderstorms grow out of such cold and warm air collisions, some becoming tornadoes. Most tornadoes happen in late spring and early summer in the central and southeastern states.

Typically these storms form on a hot summer day. Cumulus clouds gather overhead and soon turn black as the wind increases. A dark cone-shaped tail drops silently down from the clouds. The huge, hollow funnel zigzags along the ground like a giant vacuum cleaner. In its path, whatever it touches on the ground is sucked up and damaged or destroyed. The tornado's suction can cause buildings to explode, pluck feathers from chickens, and even drive straw into cows.

Project

Create a tornado tube and observe a miniature tornado vortex.

Directions

1. Fill one bottle ⅔ full with water.
2. Put a few drops of food coloring in the water and shake to mix.
3. Balance the second bottle on top of the first, neck openings together, and tape firmly.
4. Turn the bottles over, spin, and observe a tornado appear!

Materials

- Two empty plastic liter bottles
- Food coloring
- Tape
- Water

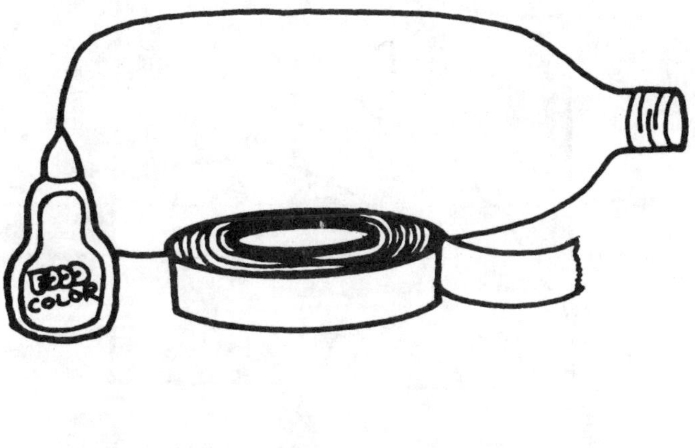

Earth's Greenhouse

Information

The sun's energy supplies Earth with heat, light, power, and weather. Without the sun there would be no life on Earth. Plants use sunlight to make their own food and to give off oxygen. Man and animals eat the plants, breathe in the oxygen, and breathe out carbon dioxide, which plants combine with energy from sunlight and ground water to produce more food.

All plants and animals living here depend on the "glass walls" of Earth's greenhouse to let in the right amount of sunlight, to block out much of the harmful rays, and to trap just enough warmth, like a cozy blanket. That blanket, our atmosphere, maintains just the right temperature and is made up of just the right mixture of gases needed by plants and animals.

But what if our "blanket" began to wear so thin that it had holes near the top and bottom of it? People around the world are thinking about just that!

Project

Make posters about Earth's changing atmosphere and climate, the greenhouse effect, ozone holes, and acid rain.

Directions

1. Divide the class into cooperative groups. Ask each group to choose one topic from the list:
   - greenhouse effect
   - ozone holes
   - acid rain
2. Research and discuss the growing problems in the Earth's atmosphere and how each relates to the weather.
3. On poster board, create a visual way of explaining what the problem is and how we might help to solve it.
4. Have each group share their poster with the class. Display the posters.

Materials

- *Our Global Greenhouse* (see Literature List, page 5)
- Poster board
- Pencil
- Scissors
- Marking pens
- Colored paper

The Water Cycle

Information

While the Earth's water supply is always moving, the amount of water stays the same. We call this the *water cycle* because the steps make a never-ending circle that carries water around the world in the form of clouds.

(1) The sun's heat changes water into vapor *(evaporation)* which rises, cools, and collects around bits of dust to form a high fog we call clouds *(condensation)*.

(2) Depending upon the temperature, the water drops fall to Earth as rain, sleet, hail, or snow.

(3) This water filters through the soil, or runs down streams into rivers, ponds, lakes or oceans, only to evaporate again. Water absorbed by plants returns to the air through a process called *transpiration.*

Project

Create a large interactive water cycle bulletin board to discuss, to chart daily temperature and precipitation, and to display students' weather projects.

Materials

- White butcher paper
- Crayons (use the sides)
- Tempera paints and brushes

Directions

1. On butcher paper, create a mural that includes the following:
   - a large sea
   - lowlands rising up to mountains: streams and rivers running downhill back to the sea
   - underground water filtering down through the soil and rocks into *aquafirs* (underground layers of porous rock, etc. containing water)
   - a few plants and animals
   - drylands on the far side of the mountains
2. Show mist evaporating from the sea, the soil, the running water, and the plants and animals (not from the drylands).
3. Color a variety of clouds, including thunderheads bumping into the mountains and dropping rain before thinning out as they go over the top and on to the drylands.

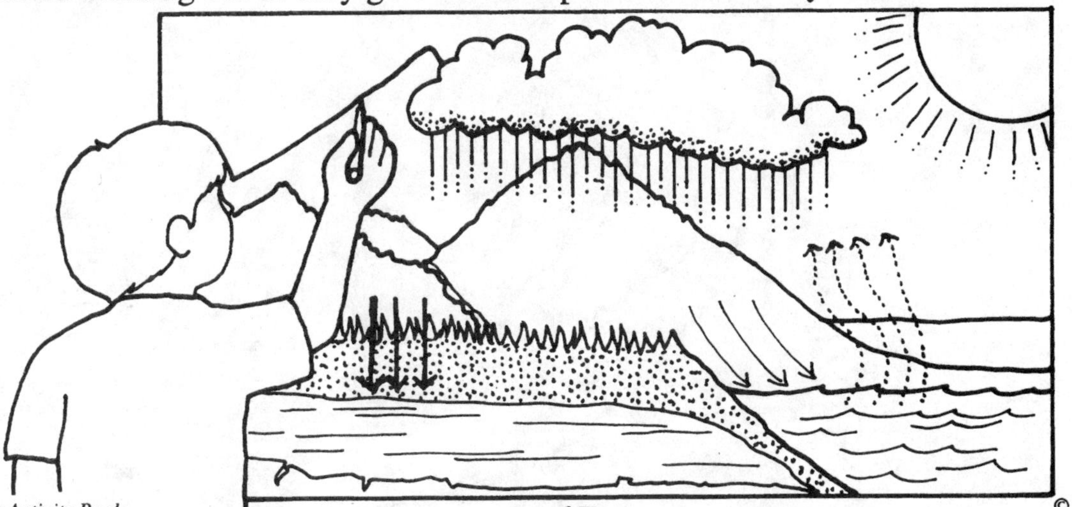

Water Cycle Wheel

Project

Make a water cycle wheel.

Materials

- Poster board
- Small brad
- Colored pencils
- Scissors

Directions

1. Color pictures.
2. Cut out the small circle and the larger cloud.
3. Cut small window out of cloud.
4. Put cloud on top of circle, matching center dots. Fasten with a brad through the center dots.
5. Turn the wheel, reading sentences 1, 2, and 3. Then put the wheel aside and retell the water cycle from memory.

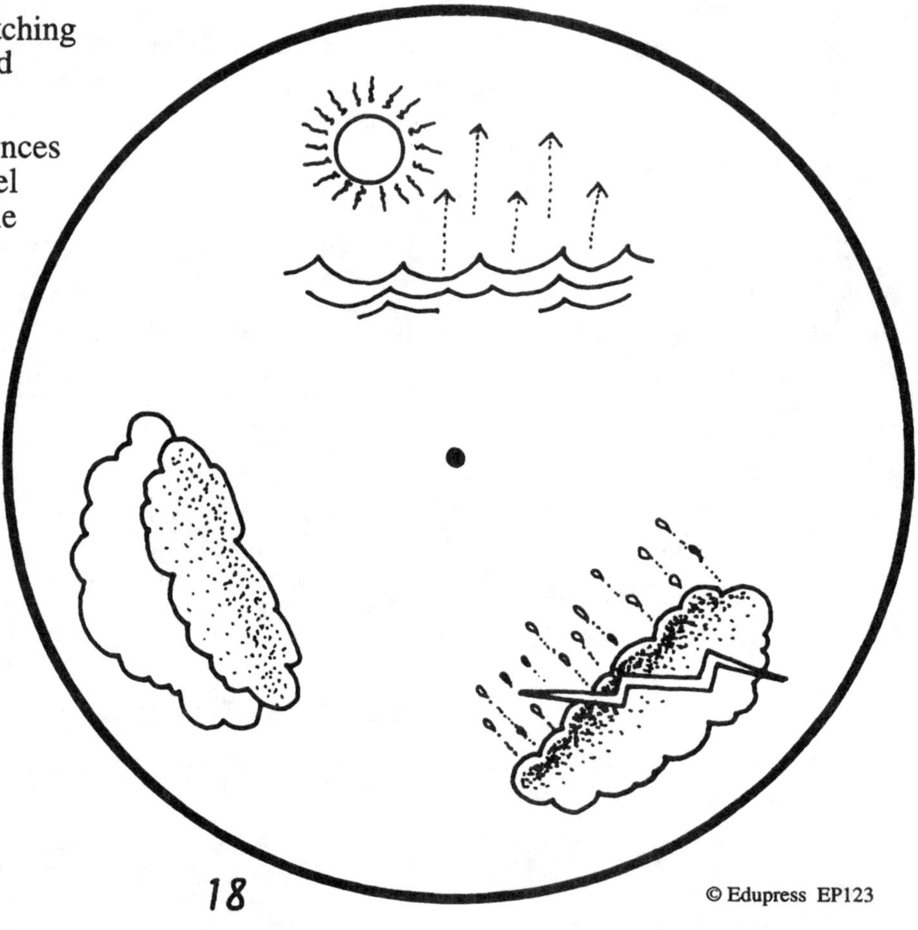

Water Cycle Wheel

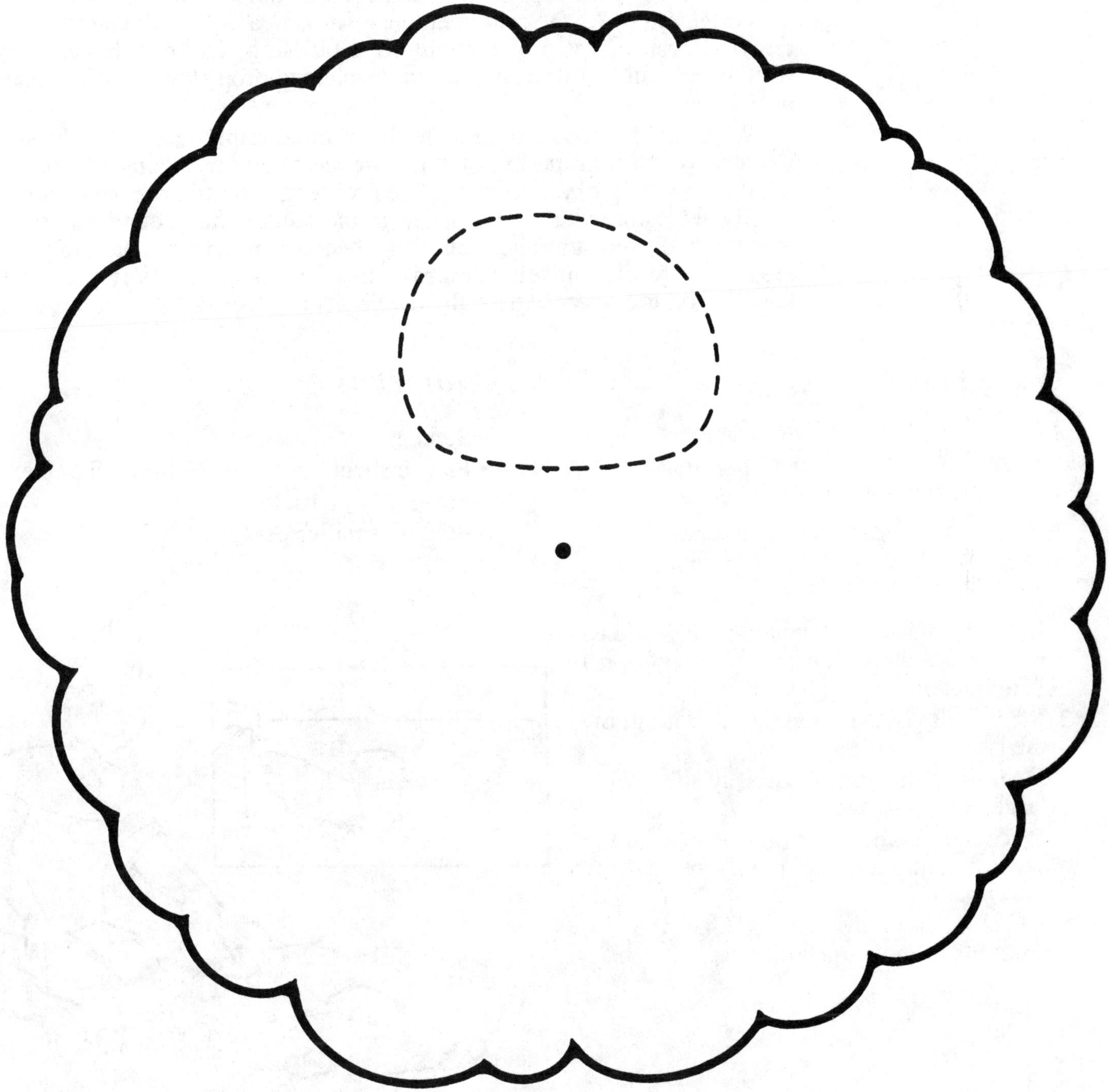

Floods and Droughts

Information

Rainstorms that drop too much water at one time or over a long period of time can cause deadly destruction over large areas of land. Once the ground has soaked up all the water it can hold and the rivers have filled up to the tops of the banks, floods begin to spread out across the countryside. As the rain continues, waters can cover the streets of a city and destroy years of planning and building. The people can only wait for the rains to stop and the floodwaters to drop slowly back to their normal levels.

When an area that is used to getting normal rainfall suddenly doesn't get any over a long period of time, we say they are having a drought. While too much rain is a destructive problem, too little rain can also be deadly. Moisture that is normally found under the ground's surface eventually disappears. The ground can become dry and too hard to grow crops. The fertile top soil can turn to dust that blows away in the wind, leaving soil too poor to grow the next season's crops.

Project

Make a survival water trap to learn about moisture found under the ground.

Materials

- Sand area
- Plastic sheet, three feet (1 m) in diameter
- Several large rocks
- Several smaller pebbles
- Cup

Directions

1. Dig a cone-shaped hole in the sand at least two feet (61 cm) deep and three feet (1 m) in diameter.
2. Place a cup in the center at the bottom of the hole.
3. Over the hole, anchor a plastic sheet with large rocks and sand.
4. Place one smaller rock in the center of the sheet, causing it to dip down directly over the cup.
5. Check often to measure and chart the amounts of moisture collected.

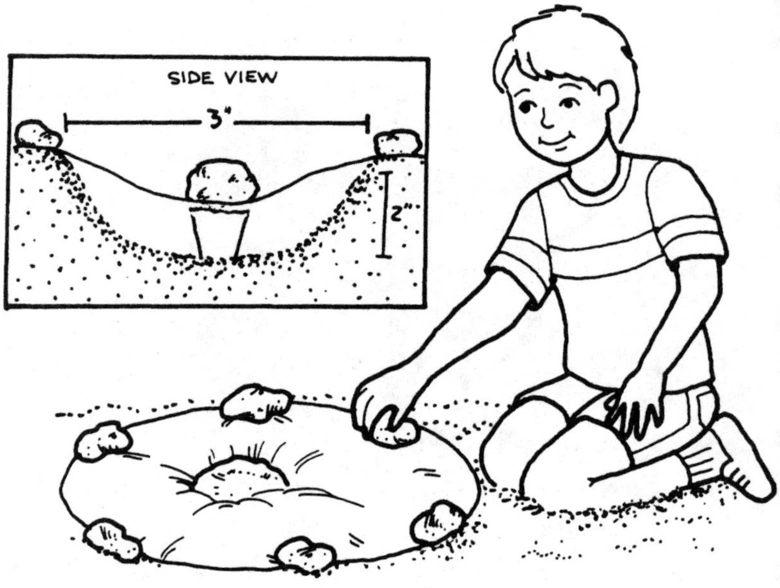

Precipitation

Information

Moisture may remain in the air as water vapor (humidity) or it falls to Earth in one of four forms of precipitation—rain, hail, sleet, or snow. When water vapor collects around dust particles, it forms tiny droplets or ice crystals. If these are high in the air, they are called clouds. If near the Earth, they form fog.

Rain is water vapor collected together until it is heavy enough to fall to Earth. Hailstones begin high in the storm clouds as tiny frozen raindrops that pick up layers of moisture as they are repeatedly tossed high in the air. Layer upon layer, they grow until they are heavy enough to fall. Sleet begins as very cold raindrops that fall through the cold air, colliding and freezing together into beads of solid ice. To see if an ice ball is hail or sleet, cut it in half. Is it layered or solid ice?

Project

Conduct precipitation experiments.

Materials

- Tea kettle
- Cold spoon
- Oven mitt
- Soap mixture
- Bubble blower

Directions

Experiment one: Create water vapor.

Adult supervision required at all times.

1. Put water in the tea kettle and bring to a boil.
2. Use an oven mitt to protect hands.
3. Hold a cold spoon in the steam and observe what happens.
4. Describe what you see happening.

Experiment two: Create water crystals.

1. Take bubble blower and soap outside in very cold weather where there is no wind.
2. Blow a large bubble very gently but make it stay on the blower wire.
3. As the bubble freezes watch for tiny ice crystals to form on the surface to make a delicate ice crystal ball.

Snow

Information

Snow is formed in cold, damp, heavy clouds. Before the water vapor can change into rain, the moisture freezes around bits of dust in the icy air and grows into tiny ice crystals. Each crystal has six sharp edges and six corners. These flakes of snow drift downward, swirling and twirling in the wind. Soon the snowflakes cover the ground with a blanket of white and pile up into snowdrifts. The dry snow that falls in very cold weather does not pack as well as the wetter snow that falls when it's not so cold.

A blizzard is a very powerful snowstorm that combines cold air, strong winds, and heavy snowfall that swirls blinding snow in the wind, piles snowdrifts against buildings, and sometimes traps people inside their homes for days.

Project

Create several kinds of unique snowflakes to hang from the classroom ceiling.

Materials

- Fishing line
- See projects, following page

Directions

1. Select one or more of the snowflake projects on the following page.
2. Fasten lengths of fishing line to the snowflakes for hanging.

Snow

Cut Paper Snowflake

Materials

- Scissors • White paper
- Small bowl or other round template
- Pencil

Directions

1. Use pencil and bowl to trace a circle on the white paper and cut out.
2. Fold the circle in half evenly, and then again to form a quarter circle.
3. Snip little pieces out of the folded edges of the paper, as shown. Open carefully.

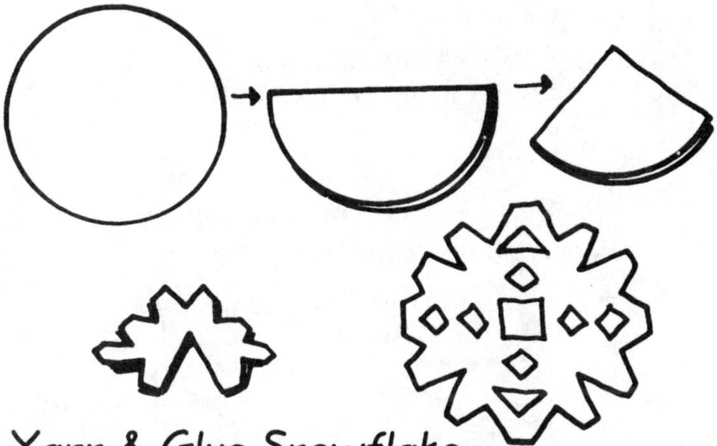

Drinking Straw Snowflake

Materials

- Scissors • Drinking straws
- Glue • Aluminum foil
- White or silver glitter

Directions

1. Cut straw into ¼-inch (.64-cm) sections.
2. Using aluminum foil as a base, glue the straw pieces together in a snowflake design.
3. Cover snowflake surface with a thin layer of glue. While still wet, sprinkle with glitter.
4. Let dry, then peel away aluminum foil.

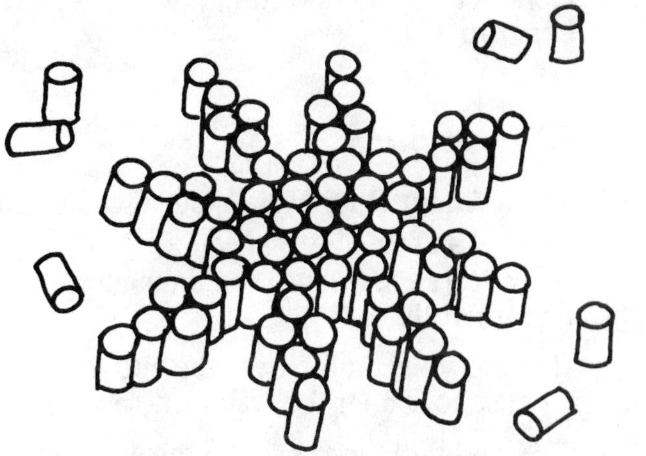

Yarn & Glue Snowflake

Materials

- Snowflake pattern, previous page
- Scissors • Paper
- White rug yarn • Glue
- Plastic bag

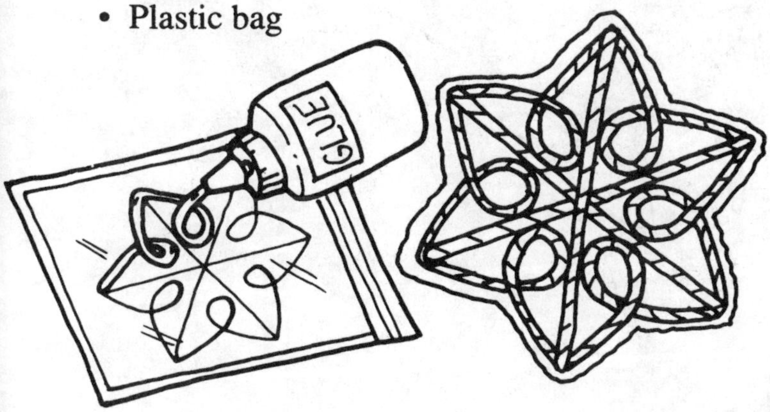

Directions

1. Trace pattern onto paper and cut out.
2. Place cutout inside the plastic bag and lay flat on a table.
3. Following the pattern, make an outline of glue on the plastic wrap. Press yarn into the glue and allow to dry.
4. Cover the entire area within outline with glue.
5. Let it dry until tacky, and spread another thin coat of glue.
6. Peel the snowflake off the plastic just before it is completely dry.

Rainbow

Information

If the sun is shining on a shower of rain you may see a rainbow. A rainbow appears only if the sun is shining through the raindrops. The almost-white sunlight breaks up into a *spectrum* of colors which scatter into a spectacular arch across the sky—red, orange, yellow, green, blue, indigo, and violet (easily remembered with the man's name: ROY G. BIV). Occasionally, a lighter second rainbow can be seen above the original bow.

A rainbow is actually a "rain-circle." Airline passengers and mountain climbers tell of seeing the complete circle of rainbow colors below them. We can see only the top half from the ground. Rainbows are seen in the mist of a waterfall, the splash of a large water fountain, or the spray of an ocean wave.

Project

Conduct two outdoor rainbow experiments.

Materials

- Garden hose
- Dishwashing soap
- Loop of thin wire or bubble wand
- Cup

Directions

Experiment One: Make your own rainbow with a garden hose.

1. Pick a sunny day. Turn the water on forcefully.
2. Hold your thumb over the end of the hose to scatter the water into a spray.
3. Stand with your back to the sun and move the spray of water to see the rainbow.
4. Explain how the rainbow is formed in the spray.

Experiment Two: Find the spectrum colors in bubbles.

1. Add a little soap to water in a cup.
2. Blow the soapy water through the loop or bubble wand and watch for rainbows in the bubbles.
3. Explain how the rainbow is formed in the bubbles.

Thunderstorms

Information

During a thunderstorm you always see the lightning before you hear the thunder. Why? Lightning is a brilliant electric spark that streaks across the sky. Because it is hot, it splits the air with a tremendous CRACK! Then the air rumbles and tumbles back together again in what we call thunder.

Lightning does not always look the same. *Fork lightning* branches into several forked paths. *Ribbon lightning* makes a flat, curling path in the sky. *Pearl lightning* is round points of very bright light strung together. The rare *ball lightning* can shoot right into a building only to explode harmlessly after a few seconds. From their spacecraft, astronauts discovered little bubbles of lightning erupting above the clouds.

Lightning skips around and flashes in all parts of a storm, not just on the leading or trailing edge. Counting seconds to determine the distance lightning is from you may give a false sense of security. The next bolt might be right next to you. If you can hear thunder, you can be hit by lightning.

Project

Learn to count seconds accurately to determine how far away lightning is from you.

Materials

- Flashlight (optional)
- Clock with second hand

Directions

You can tell how close lightning is by counting the seconds between the flash and the sound of thunder. Sound travels about one mile in five seconds.

1. Count five seconds slowly, "One thunder, two thunder, three thunder, four thunder, five thunder." That's a mile away. Counting ten seconds between the flash and the rumble means the lightning is about two miles away.
2. Divide class into two teams. Take turns creating and timing the light and the sound of thunder.
3. Make lightning flashes in a dark room with the light switch or a bright flashlight. Make the sound of thunder by stomping feet. Use the second hand on the clock to check accuracy and judge how fast to count.

Saint Elmo's Fire

Information

Picture a ship at sea in stormy weather, thunder rumbling, lightning streaking across the sky. Sailors suddenly see a ghostly, glowing light around the ship's masts. "Look there! It's Saint Elmo's Fire!" they shout.

Saint Elmo's Fire was once thought to be folklore—a sailor's tall tale of his journey at sea. Today sailors know that Saint Elmo's Fire is a kind of electricity that won't burn or hurt them. During a storm, electricity in the air moves into the ship. As the ship sails along electricity builds up until the ship can't hold any more. The stored-up electricity suddenly shoots back up into the air in a round flash of eerie light.

Sometimes Saint Elmo's Fire can be seen dancing from high towers, church steeples, and even around airplanes. It has been reported to flicker along a horse's mane or glow around a person's head without them even knowing it.

Project

Combine a popular artists' technique of pen and ink with crayon resist to paint a picture of Saint Elmo's Fire. Create a ship's log to record ocean weather.

Materials

- Black ink and pens **or** thin black marking pens
- White and black construction paper
- Watercolor paints and brushes
- Crayons
- Scissors
- Glue
- Ship's Log pattern page, following

Directions

1. Use pen and ink or a thin black marking pen to draw a picture of a tall-masted sailing ship on a sheet of white construction paper.
2. Press heavily with crayons to color between the pen lines of the picture.
3. With crayon, add the yellowish-white light of Saint Elmo's Fire bursting around the masts and upper ship.
4. Cover the entire paper with a watercolor wash. Allow it to dry.
5. Cut out the ship and glue it to a sheet of black construction paper.
6. Reproduce the ship's log pattern to create a log in which the effects of weather at sea are described through the eyes of a sailor.

Ship's Log

Storm Safety

Information

It is important to know the dangers of different types of storms and to understand the storm warnings. For tornadoes, often little or no warning is given. Hurricane warnings are given early but many people fail to heed them. Lightning bolts strike without warning. Be aware that lightning is the number two killer after fires and that more children are killed by lightning than adults. Most important to know is how to get to a safe shelter at the first hint of danger. Don't delay!

Project

Discuss the three types of dangerous storms and conduct storm safety drills.

Local officials issue advisories if a hurricane is approaching land. It is best to board up property and simply leave the area as soon as possible, getting far enough away to avoid high winds and the potential danger of a storm surge. Because flooding often occurs in low coastal areas, your house and especially a cellar is not a safe shelter. Plan ahead and make arrangements where you can go. Tune in to **local** radio and television stations for information on the hurricane's progress and where to go to be safe. Plan to stay some distance away with relatives and friends, or call your local Red Cross for the nearest evacuation shelter to wait out the storm.

Drill

Role-play boarding up houses, traveling to a safe spot, and waiting out the storm. Discuss possible activities, fears, sleeping and eating arrangements, returning home after the storm.

At the first warning or sight of a tornado, get your radio and seek shelter in a storm cellar or basement. Crouch in the southwest corner to protect yourself from the debris that usually swirls and falls in the northeast corner. In buildings with no basement, go to the lowest level to an interior room with no windows like a closet or bathroom. Sit facing the wall, covering the head and neck with hands. Remain there until you hear the radio give the "all clear."

Drill

Conduct a tornado drill. Announce there has been a tornado warning. Line up and walk quietly to the interior hallway of the school. Sit bent over facing the wall with head and neck covered with hands. Keep eyes tightly closed if the wind whips through the hallway. Listen for directions. Wait for the "all-clear" signal before returning to the classroom.

If you hear thunder, lightning is close enough to strike you. Immediately **get inside a building.** If you cannot get to a shelter, move into the most open area away from trees and metal objects and crouch low over your feet. Get away from water. Water is an excellent conductor of electricity, making your chances of electrical shock quite high. Get back to shore and off boats as soon as possible.

Drills

Start on the playground. Move in orderly lines and get inside the school building as quickly and quietly as possible. Start again on the playground and this time, pretend there is no shelter nearby. Move to an open area. Have the children crouch low in a ball position over their feet to be in as little contact with the ground as possible. Do not lie on the ground!

Weather Forecasting

Information

All over the world weather experts, known as *meteorologists,* gather and share information about weather conditions, using many tools and instruments to measure and record weather.

Wind speed and wind direction are the key to describing and predicting weather. Wind direction is measured most simply by a wind vane or a windsock, but can be measured also by helium-filled balloons called *radiosonders*. The tool called a sunshine recorder measures daily hours of sunshine. The thermometer measures the temperature of the air, and the rain gauge measures the amount of rain that has fallen. Weather aircraft, ships, and satellites feed photos and information into powerful computers which plot weather and reveal weather patterns.

Project

Begin to build a forecasting station by creating and experimenting with models of the forecasting tools shown on following pages.

Materials

- Listed with projects on the following pages

Directions

1. Divide the class into small cooperative groups.
2. Each group selects the weather forecasting tool they will make and demonstrate and gathers the materials needed to complete their project.
3. Groups report back to class, explaining and demonstrating their working model.

Rain Gauge

Information

The air in Earth's atmosphere is seldom dry. It usually contains a gas form of water we call *vapor,* which is invisible. When this water vapor condenses (turns to liquid), it forms tiny droplets of water which we see as clouds, low fog, or mist. When these water droplets get large and heavy enough, they fall to Earth as rain.

Meteorologists measure the amount of rainfall with a rain gauge. The rain gauge measures the depth of water that would occur if the rain did not drain away. It measures rain that has fallen in a particular spot. Rainfall is measured in inches or millimeters. Experts chart and average the rainfall year after year.

Project

Make a simple rain gauge and record the daily amounts of rain for a month.

Materials

- Large jar with a neck
- Funnel—size to fit neck of jar
- Square of stiff foam plastic
- Small ruler
- Calendar
- Pencil

Directions

1. Cut a small hole in the center of the foam plastic.
2. Push the funnel spout into the hole.
3. In an area open to the sky, bury the jar in the ground with its neck at ground level.
4. Place the plastic over the jar with the funnel spout extending down into the jar.
5. Each day, remove the jar and measure the water level inside.
6. Record the amount on a calendar.
7. Empty out that day's water before replacing the jar in the ground.

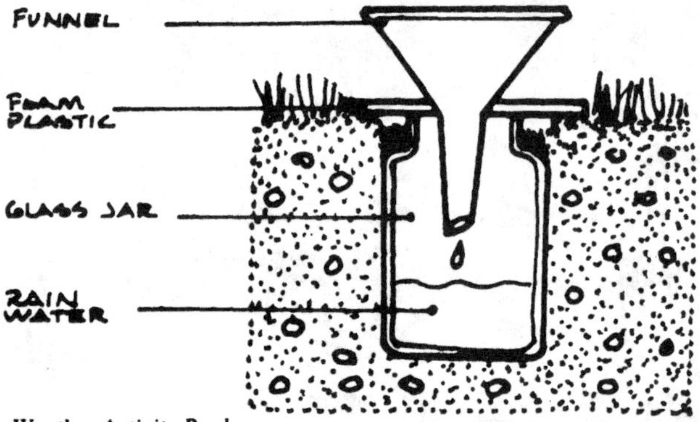

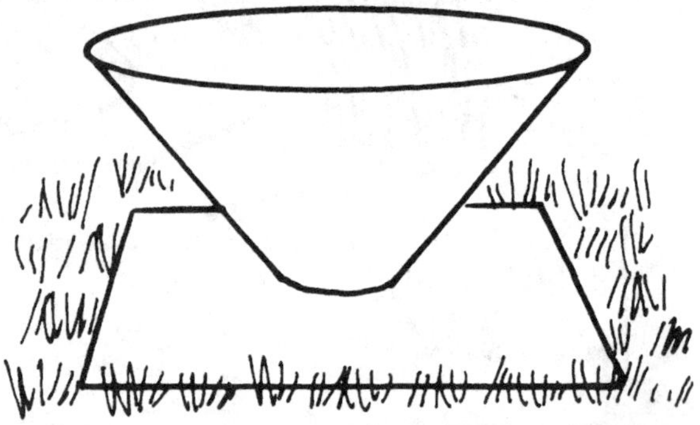

Barometer

Information

Most of Earth's air is concentrated about three miles (5 km) above Earth. We feel water pressure when swimming deep underwater. Likewise, the atmosphere (air around us) presses 14 pounds (6.35 kg) on each square inch of our skin. Our body is so accustomed to it, we don't notice.

Barometers measure air pressure. Weathermen use a mercury barometer, a long glass tube with its open end standing in mercury, which rises as the air pressure changes. They use a scale marked in millibars (one-one-thousandth of a bar). The mercury barometer readings must be corrected for variations in temperature, gravity, and altitude differences.

Project

Create a barometer and chart the pushing power of air for a period of time.

Materials

- Clear plastic liter bottle
- Bowl of water
- Paper
- Tape
- Ruler
- Index card
- Modeling clay
- String

Directions

1. Use clay to hold the ruler upright at one side of the bowl.
2. Fill the bottle three-fourths full of water and the bowl about three inches (8 cm) full.
3. Covering the top with your hand, invert the bottle and stand it in the bowl, under water.
4. Remove your hand, but hold the bottle upright while you tie it to the ruler with string.
5. Mark a milliliter scale on the index card and tape it to the side of the bottle.

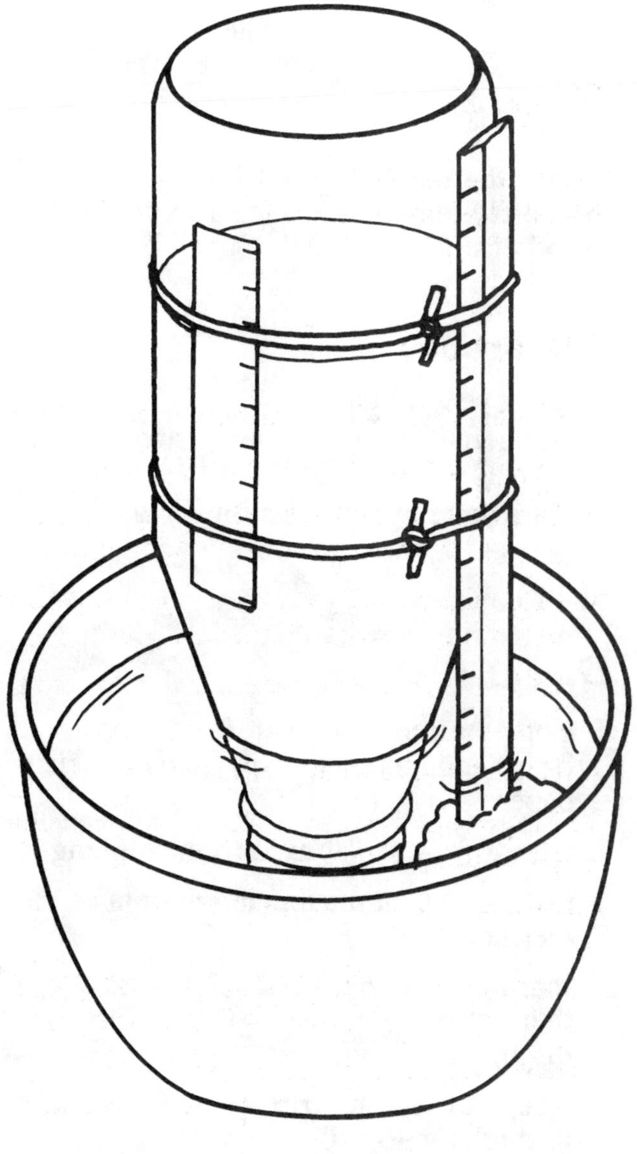

Thermometer

Information

Air temperature, the degree of heat or cold in the air, is measured by a thermometer. The most commonly used is the mercury-in-glass thermometer. It is easy to make, easy to read, reliable, convenient, cheap, and it requires no maintenance. When the temperature goes up, the mercury rises in the tube. When the temperatures are expected to go below the freezing point of mercury, an alcohol thermometer is used.

Temperature is measured by the Celsius scale or the Fahrenheit scale. The Fahrenheit scale has 180 divisions between the freezing point of water (32ºF) and the boiling point of water (212ºF). The Celsius scale has 100 divisions between the freezing point of water (0ºC) and the boiling point of water (100ºC) at sea level.

Thermometers are also used to take a person's temperature to see if they have a fever and to insure our food is prepared and stored properly.

Project

Make a thermometer model and chart daily temperatures for a short period of time.

Materials

- Heavy poster board
- Thermometer and mercury strips pattern, following page
- White and red construction paper
- Scissors
- Glue

Directions

1. Copy thermometer pattern onto poster board and mercury strips onto construction paper.
2. Glue Tab A to Tab B to form one long strip.
3. Cut the slits at the top and bottom of the thermometer.
4. Starting with the * end behind the thermometer, slide the mercury strip through the bottom slit.
6. Keep pulling the strip up the front and through the top slit.
7. Move the mercury up and down by holding on to the strip underneath.

Thermometer Pattern

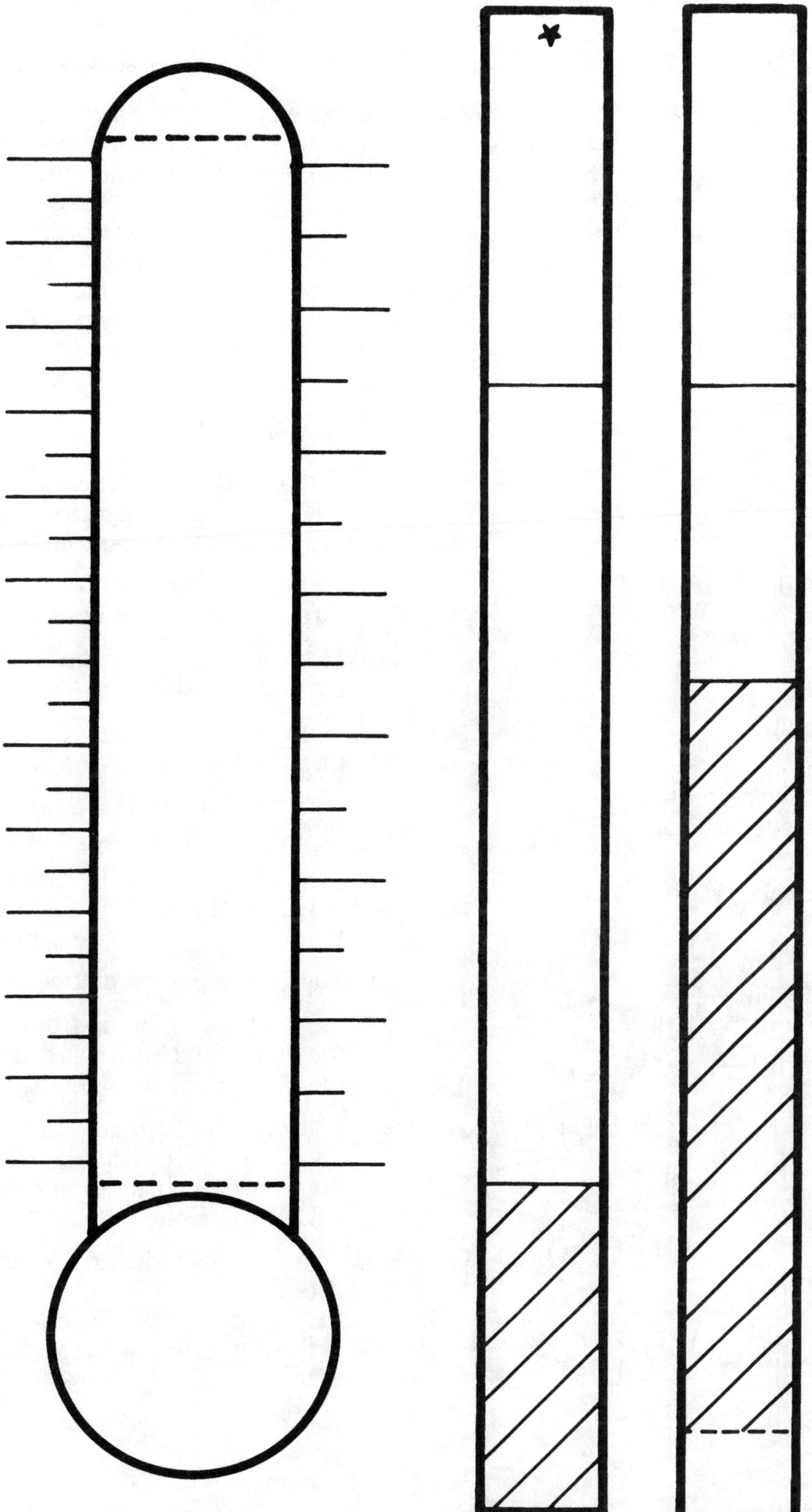

Anemometer

Information

Anemometers measure the speed of the wind. An anemometer is an instrument that has three or four cups attached to rods that are two to eight inches (5 to 20 cm) long. They rotate on a vertical spindle. The wind makes the cups spin around regardless of the wind direction. Weather experts can calculate wind speed from the speed at which the cups are moving. The wind speed is measured by the number of revolutions the cups make in a given time period. Wind speeds in the United States are stated in knots or miles per hour. One knot is equal to 1.15 (1.85 km) miles per hour.

Project

Create an anemometer and record wind speeds for one week.

Materials

- Four paper cups
- Thumbtack
- Empty ballpoint pen tube
- Two thin pieces of wood
- Paper towel tube
- Small ball of clay
- Shoebox
- Tape
- Stones
- Pin
- Thread

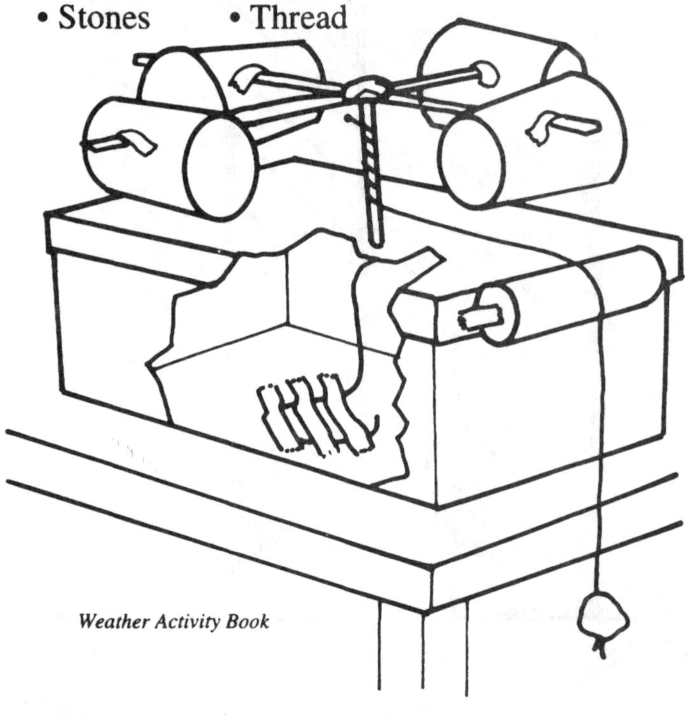

Directions

1. Cut a section of wire and make a loop at one end. Bend the loop at a 45° angle as a base and tape to the inside bottom of the box.
2. Add stones for stability and put the lid on the box, pushing the wire through the lid.
3. Make a cross out of the wood pieces and tape securely.
4. With cups facing the same way, push wood through the sides of the cups and tape to hold.
5. Using a thumbtack and tape, attach the flat end of the pen tube to the center of the wood cross.
6. Insert the wire into the pen tube, adding a small pin through the tiny hole as a stop. The wire should rotate easily in the wind.
7. Tape the paper towel tube to one end of the lid.
8. Tie a length of thread from the small pin. Knot the untied end of the thread, and attach a ball of clay to provide weight.
9. Place the anemometer on a table outside in a windy spot, allowing the weighted thread to drape over the paper towel tube and down the side of the table.
10. As the cups blow around and wind the string, notice how long it takes for the weight to rise to the edge of the table. Record the wind speed in different winds several times a day.

Weather Vane

Information

Weathermen use a weather vane to determine the wind's direction. Rooster-shaped weather vanes are often found on barns to help farmers predict weather on their own. The vane has a flat, wide blade attached to a spoke pivoted at one end. The wind turns the blade on the spoke to line it up with 360° marks on a circle. North is at 0°, east is at 90°, south is at 180°, and west is at 270°.

Forecasters always speak of the direction the wind as *coming from.* Knowing a west wind blows *from* the west allows them to predict more accurately what the weather will be.

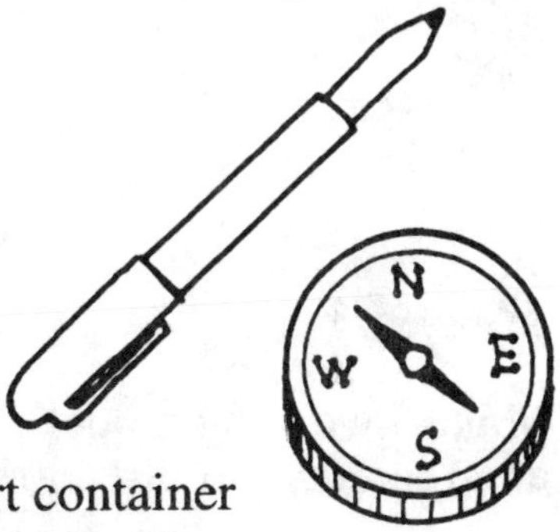

Project

Create a weather vane and chart the wind direction for a short period of time.

Materials

- Empty yogurt container
- Pencil with eraser
- Modeling clay
- Board about 10 x 10 x ½ inches (25 x 25 x 1.27 cm)
- Index card
- Glue
- Straight pin
- Marking pen
- Drinking straw
- Scissors
- Compass

Directions

1. Push the pencil through the center of the bottom of the yogurt container.
2. Cut a slit in each end of the straw. Cut two triangles from the index card. Glue one to each slit end of the straw.
3. Stick a blob of clay on the pencil point. Use clay around the carton's edge to anchor it to the center of the board. Push pencil down to attach the clay on the pencil point to the board.
4. Insert the pin all the way through the center of the straw and into the eraser.
5. Place the weather vane on a flat spot in an open area.
6. Use the compass and marking pen to mark north, south, east, and west on the container. Check several times a day as the wind changes, and record the wind direction.

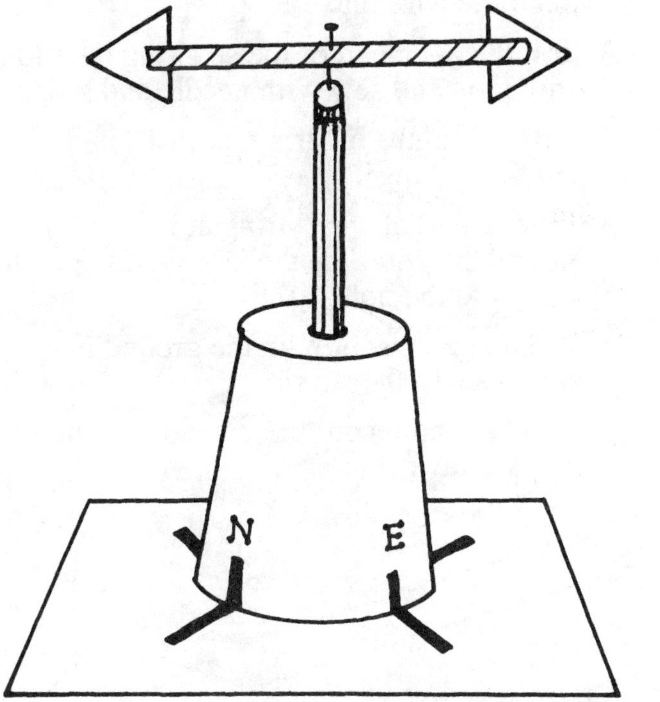

Windsock

Information

Windsocks are used to show the direction of the wind. They are seen at airports, seaports, and along especially windy mountain roads or areas exposed to strong winds. The windsock swivels on a pole away from the wind, thus allowing the wind to blow into its open "mouth." The wind is blowing in the direction the tail of the sock is pointing. A loosely flapping sock means a light wind is blowing. A stiff straight sock means a strong wind.

Project

Make a working model of a windsock and record wind direction.

Materials

- Nylon stocking
- Thin wire
- Wood or bamboo pole
- Thin string
- Needle with a large eye

Directions

1. Cut off a two-foot (61-cm) piece from the lower part of the stocking leg.
2. Bend the wire into a loop.
3. Roll the open end of the stocking over the wire loop and sew with needle and string.
4. Cut six lengths of string, each 12 inches (30.5 cm) long.
5. Tie one end of each string at intervals around the wire. Tie the loose ends of all the strings to the pole.
6. Sink the pole solidly in the ground in an area open to the wind.
7. Observe and record the wind direction three times a day.

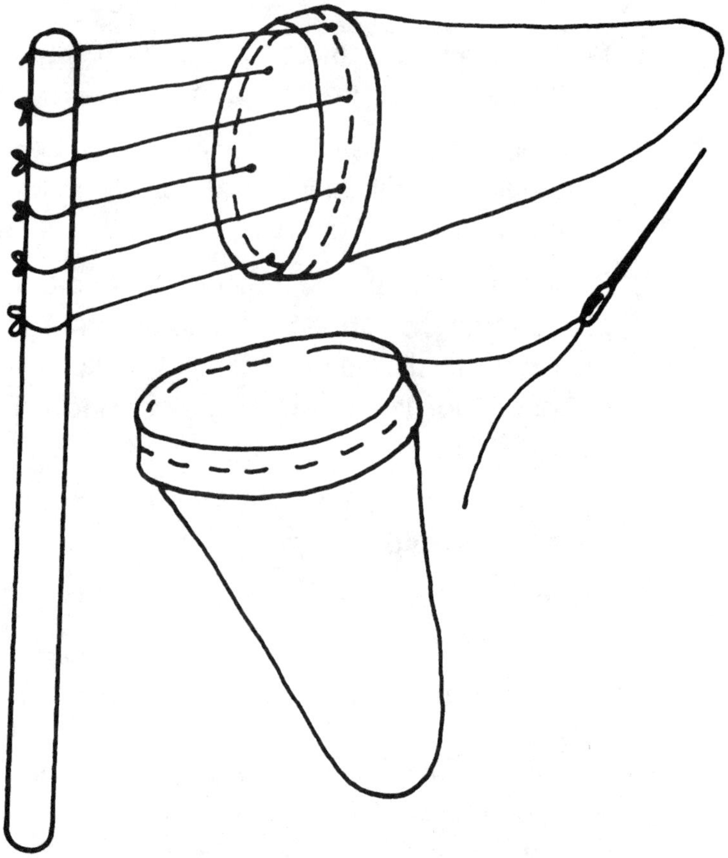

Weather Reporting

Information

Forecasting the weather involves analyzing various types of computer-generated maps and charts. Forecast maps predict the temperature, air pressure, wind direction and speed, humidity and precipitation. A temperature chart indicates the highest and lowest surface temperature over a 24-hour period. A precipitation chart tells where precipitation occurred during the same period.

There are two kinds of forecasts—short-range and extended. Short range forecasts make predictions for the next 18 to 36 hours and are updated several times a day. Extended forecasts predict the weather over the next five days and the following six to ten days. These are updated three times a week. Forecasts, reports, and warnings are shared with the public by means of newspapers, radio broadcasts, and television newscasts. These same media systems, plus magazines and the world wide web, also bring weather-related news events and current information to the public.

Project

Become familiar with the different ways the media informs the public about weather predictions and weather-related stories. Participate in related activities.

Materials

- Radio and televison
- Paper, pencil, poster board, and other materials required by each cooperative group to complete their newscast
- Video camera (optional)

Directions

1. Spend some time listening to and watching weather reports on television. This can be accomplished during class or at home.
2. Discuss the format and information that was shared.
3. Divide the class into small cooperative groups of three to four students each.
4. Direct each group to select either a radio or television weather forecast to simulate.
5. Each group is responsible for assembling costumes, creating charts, writing scripts and incorporating weather terms. Encourage them to practice several times before broadcast day arrives.
6. Video-taping their reports adds an element of realism and allows children to see themselves on television!

Weather in the News

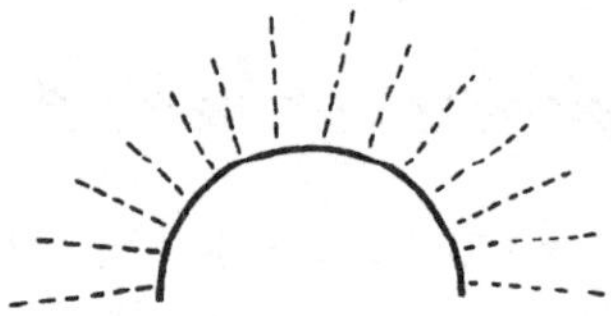

The newspaper is a great resource for weather information. Every newspaper has weather summaries plus a section devoted to local, national, and international weather.

Look here, too, for news-worthy current events and human interest stories.

Here are newspaper-based activities that allow students to compare and relate weather and its effects to the world around them.

Current Events Display

Create a bulletin board to feature weather in the news. Ask children to comb newspapers and other periodicals for stories and articles that relate to the weather and its effects.

Clip out the story and present an oral summary of its content to the rest of the class. Add the news clipping to the bulletin board.

Encourage students to brainstorm related activities in which to participate. These might include:

- Care packages for victims of weather disasters.
- Distributing weather safety information in the school or community.

Weather Page Fun

Tear out the weather section from several different newspapers.

- Study the maps and charts and learn to interpret them. Check the accuracy of the short-range and extended forecasts.
- Choose several national or international cities for weather tracking over a period of a week or month. Keep records on weather changes in that city and present the weather report to classmates.
- Find the highest and lowest temperatures on a daily basis. Use color-coded push pins (red-hottest; blue-coldest) to mark the locations on a wall-mounted map. Can any weather patterns be established?
- Make a list of the other information that is found in the weather section. Determine why it relates to the weather.

Jack Frost

Information

After a cold, starry night, early in the morning, we awake to window panes covered with sparkling, lacy-white pictures which we call "Jack Frost." This imaginary friend paints artistically with just a thin layer of ice.

Frost forms when the ground is frozen and the air is damp. Each droplet of water in the damp air is chilled, getting colder and colder, until, one at a time, they suddenly freeze on the window. The crystals of ice spread out in amazing fern-like sprays, swirling in feathery coils all across the window pane.

Project

Create a Jack Frost window.

Directions

1. Pour white paint and detergent in a pie tin.
2. Dip feather, then fern into paint. Wipe excess off on edge of pie tin.
3. Press designs onto blue paper, overlapping to give a frosted look. Allow it to dry.
4. Cut one-inch (2.54-cm) strips and mount as the window frames.
5. Cut curtains from fabric and glue on top of the window frame.
6. Write a story about Jack Frost to display with the window pane picture.

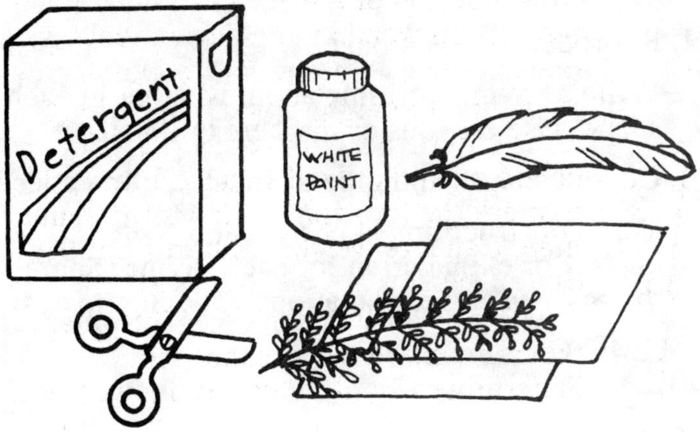

Materials

- Blue and black construction paper
- Feathers and fern leaves
- White tempera paint, watered down slightly
- Snow-like laundry detergent
- Shallow pie tin
- Fabric scraps
- Scissors
- Glue

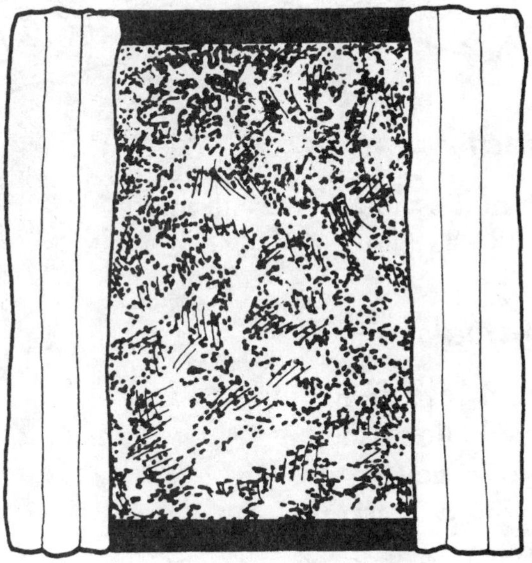

Rhymes and Riddles

Information

People have fun making up rhymes about the weather signs they observe in nature. Weather rhymes and riddles are seldom true, but some have enough truth in them to help people predict changes in the weather, or at least to help them remember weather patterns. Think about this one. "A ring around the sun or moon, brings rain or snow upon us soon." This refers to the ice crystals in high clouds that cause this ring to appear.

Rainbow at night, a sailor's delight:
Rainbow at morning, sailors take warning.

Rainbows are sunlight shining through raindrops in the sky opposite the sun. The sun appears to move east to west while rain usually moves west to east. An evening rainbow seen in the east means rain has passed. A morning rainbow seen in the west means rain is on the way.

Cow with its tail to the west
Always makes the weather best.

Cows like to stand with their tails to the wind rather than face the wind. Winds from the west are good.

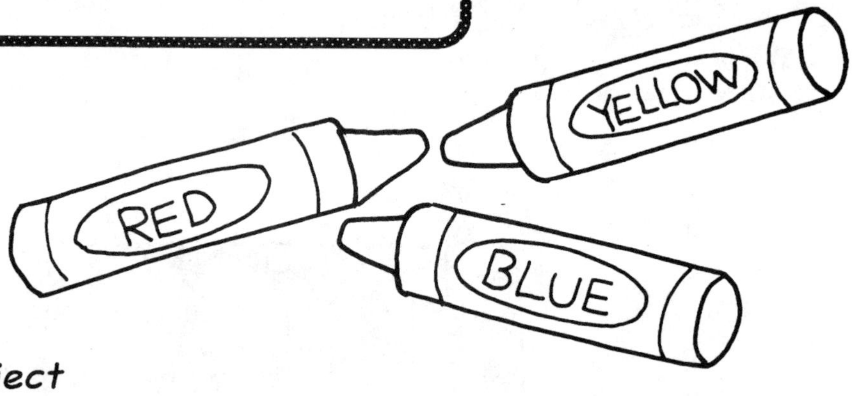

Mackerel sky,
Soon wet or dry.

Mackerel clouds look like scales on fish. They may be leftover clouds from the last storm, or they can grow into rain clouds.

Project

Create riddles and rhymes about things observed in weather.

Materials

- Pattern page, following
- Construction paper
- Pen or pencil
- Crayons or markers
- Scissors
- Glue

Directions

1. Reproduce pattern page.
2. Write a rhyme or riddle about weather in each shape. Use crayons or markers to illustrate.
3. Cut out shapes and glue to construction paper.
4. Turn construction paper over and write the answer or explanation for each rhyme. Share the rhymes and explanations with classmates.

Rhymes and Riddles

Poetry

Information

Various elements of weather have their own distinct moods which, in turn, have a strong effect on our emotions. Many writers feel compelled to express their childish delight at a gentle spring storm or rainbow, their awe at a beautiful sunset glowing on a bank of clouds, the humor of a swirling, prancing dust devil, their absolute terror at the approach of a catastrophic storm. Poetry is an excellent way to describe what we know and observe about weather because we can express our emotional reactions as well.

Project

Write weather poems to describe what has been learned in your weather study.

Directions

1. Discuss different kinds of poetry, including the examples on this page.
2. Have students select one or more poetry forms to use in creating their own poems.
3. Illustrate the poems with art media of choice, mounting each illustration with its poem on construction paper. Use the finished projects in a poetry bulletin board display.

Materials

- Writing paper
- Pencil
- Crayons or other illustration media
- Construction paper in a variety of colors
- Glue for mounting

Doublet Rhymes

Doublets are simple pairs of rhyming lines.

Raindrops in a gentle breeze
Bring the scent of distant seas.

Lightning streaks the summer sky
As winds send storm clouds rolling by.

Haiku

Haiku poems started a long time ago in the Orient. They are usually about nature. You must know how to count syllables to write Haiku. The most popular form of Haiku has three lines, with five syllables in the first line, seven syllables in the second line, and five syllables in the last.

Snow flakes all around
Falling gently to the ground,
Forming fun snow drifts.

Alphabet Poem

An alphabet poem starts with a list of the letters of the alphabet down the left-hand side of a paper. Create a weather-related phrase for each letter. They need not rhyme.

A is for air that everyone breathes.
B is for the barometer measuring air pressure.
C is for clouds that float in the sky.

Fun and Games

Information

Indoors or out, you can have fun with Weather Games! Try these activities to reinforce weather learning.

Weather Concentration

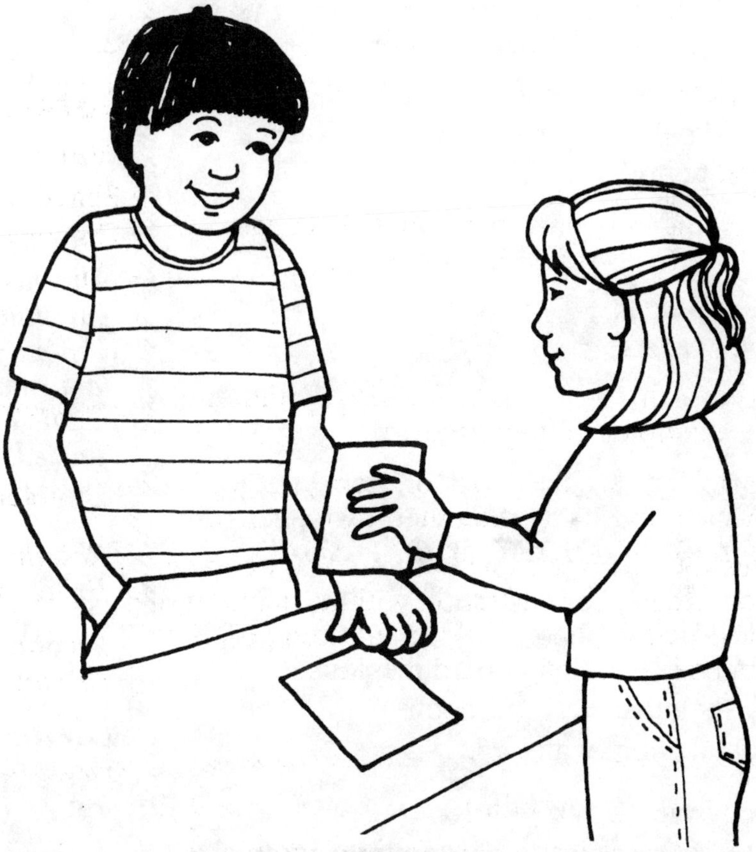

You Will Need:

Materials needed:
- Index cards
- Black marking pens
- Glossary, page 6

Directions

1. Divide the class into two teams, each team taking one column of the weather glossary words and definitions.
2. Have the members of each team use index cards to write the words on one card and the definitions on another.
3. Lay all the cards face down in rows on the floor.
4. To begin play, one player of Team 1 draws and shows two cards. If the word and the definition on those two cards match, Team 1 keeps those two cards. If not, the cards are placed back in the rows and play moves to Team 2, who draws and tries to match two cards.
5. Play continues until all of the words and definitions have been matched and taken. The team with the most cards wins.

Fun and Games

Hail Toss

You Will Need:
• One-inch (2.54 cm) Styrofoam™ balls

Directions
1. Practice juggling first by tossing one ball from one hand to the other.
2. When competent, toss a second ball when the first is to the halfway point.
3. When you get good with two balls, add a third ball and you're juggling! Keep practicing!

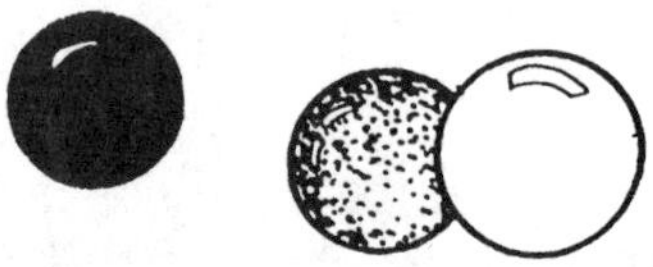

Puddle Tag

You Will Need:
• Blue yarn

Directions
1. Use blue yarn to outline puddle shapes in the game area. Select one player to be "tagger."
2. Any player standing in a puddle is safe. However, once inside a puddle a player must count to ten and move on to another puddle.
3. Players tagged become "taggers." Game continues until one player is left untagged.

Alternate Activity: Create one large puddle and challenge students to "jump" the puddle without getting their feet wet. To make the game more difficult, increase the size of the puddle or make several puddles in a row to be cleared.

Temperature Relay

You Will Need:
• Ice cubes
• Washcloths
• Hot and cold water
• Blue ice-packs
• Spoons

Directions
1. Divide glass into teams no larger than six players.
2. Have the first child on each team hold an ice cube, an ice-pack or a cold spoon and walk quickly to a designated line and back.
3. When every child on the team has played, repeat the activity with a hot washcloth or hot spoon. (Take care that hot objects are not to hot to handle.)

Snow Tag

You Will Need:
• Playing area covered with fresh snow

Directions:
1. Tramp down the pattern of a spoked wheel. Select one player to be "it."
2. "It" tries to tag the other players, but the players can run only in the pattern tramped out in the snow. (In areas with no snow, use chalk to outline a wheel-shaped path for players to use.)

Weather Treats

Information

Weather has a way of making us think in terms of food. Warm weather sends us into the garden to pick our own fruits and vegetables. Hot weather stirs us to think of ice cream and frosty drinks. Rainy days demand hot soup and hot chocolate. Snowstorms inspire us to cook the whole meal in the oven to warm up the house at the same time. Clear summer days bring the smells of outdoor barbecues.

Project

Make and sample Weather Treats.

Materials

See ingredients and equipment needed for individual recipes

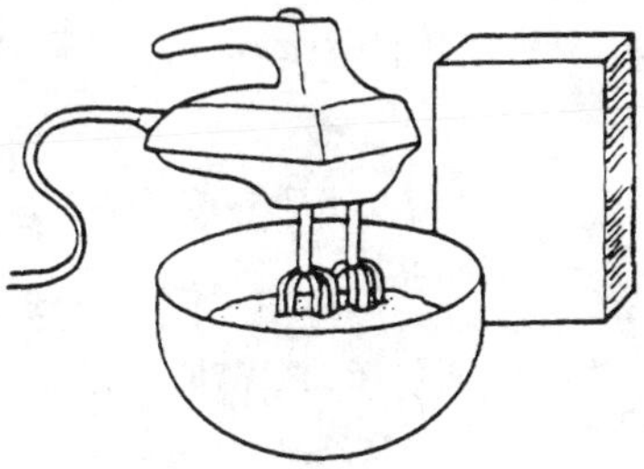

Meringue Clouds

Ingredients:
- 2 eggs
- ⅔ cup (158 ml) superfine sugar

Directions:
1. Separate egg yolks from whites.
2. Beat egg whites with an **egg beater** until they stand up stiffly in little peaks.
3. Add ⅓ cup (79 ml) of sugar to egg whites and beat again.
4. Add the rest of the sugar, folding in very gently with a **metal mixing spoon**.
5. Turn on the **oven** and set at 250°F (121°C) or lower.
6. **Oil** a piece of **aluminum foil** and place it on a **baking sheet**.
7. Spoon the meringue on the foil in the shape of small oval clouds.
8. Place clouds in oven and leave for two to three hours until they are dry. Remove carefully with a long **spatula**. Cool on a **wire rack**.

Lemon Freeze

Ingredients:
- Lemons
- Superfine sugar
- Soda water
- Ice

Directions for one serving:
1. Squeeze the juice of one lemon into a **tall glass**.
2. Add 1 tablespoon (15 ml) of sugar.
3. In a **cloth towel**, crush ice with **kitchen hammer** or use an **ice crusher.**
4. Add the ice to the lemon and sugar mixture.
5. Fill glass with soda water and serve at once with a **straw**.
6. For pink lemon freezes, add a drop of **maraschino cherry juice** or **red food coloring.**

Kites

Information

Kites are claimed to have been invented between 400 and 200 BC by both the Greeks and the Chinese. In 1749 two Scotsmen tied thermometers to a train of kites to record the temperature of clouds. They sent up the first kite and thermometer as far as the string could go, then hooked that end of the string to another kite which rose to its string's limit. More kites were added until the string snapped. As the kites rose, a slow-burning fuse burned until the thermometer dropped, trailing a white ribbon to aid in its recovery.

By the 1900s train kites recorded air pressure, wind speed, temperature, and humidity with a small *meteorograph.* Kite trains were used for sending up radar reflectors, building bridges, designing airplanes, and taking photos,

Important kite rules are: never use metal in making kites; never fly a kite near electric wires; never fly a kite in a thunderstorm or use wire or wet string for a line because of the danger of lightning. Ben Franklin's experiment with a kite, a wet string, and a key could have killed him.

Project

Make and fly a paper-bag kite.

Materials

- Large paper bag
- Clear tape
- String
- Scissors
- Pencil
- Colored marking pens
- Cloth scraps for tail (optional)

Directions

1. Cut off the bottom of the bag. Fold the sides down to make the bag flat.
2. Turn the bag over and mark the center a third of the way down.
3. Turn the bag over. Tape the points of the wings to reinforce the paper. Punch a string-hole in each taped point and add strings.
4. Cut a small vent hole near the bottom and, if desired, add a tail of cloth scraps tied to string.
5. Decorate the kite as you wish.

Kite Directions

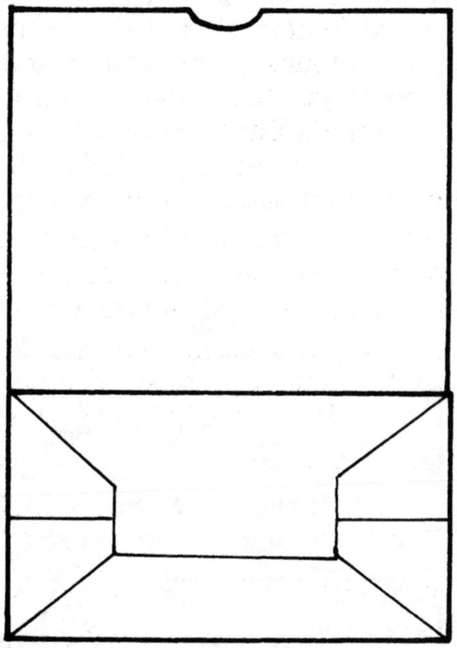

1.

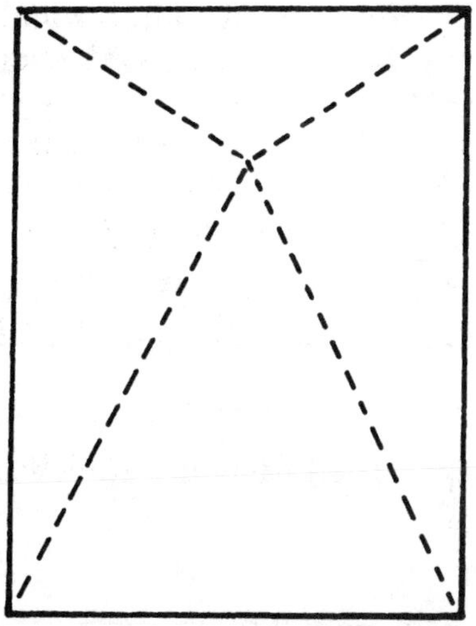

2.

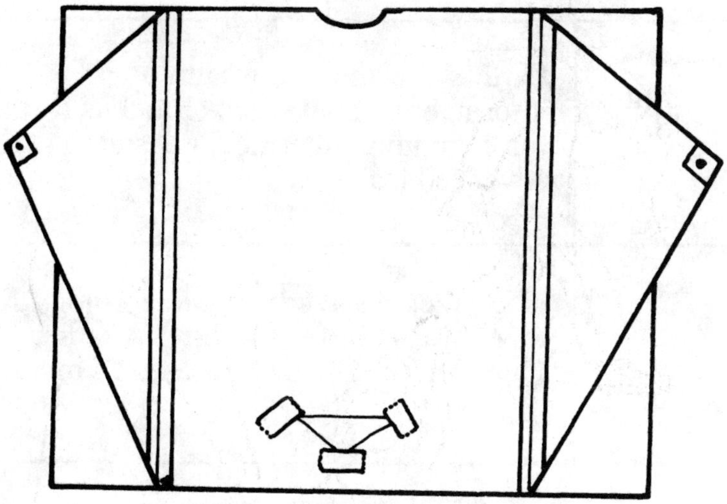

3.

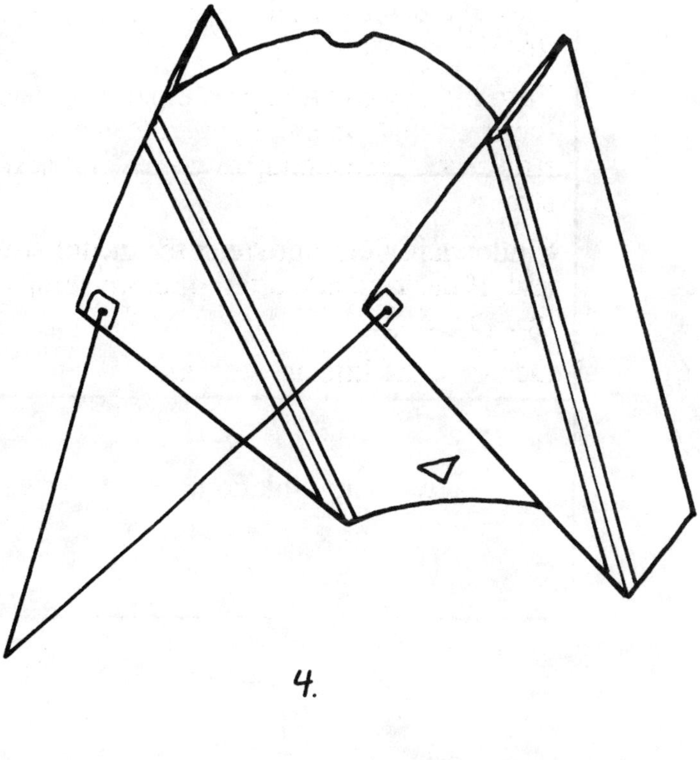

4.

World Wide Web

Look in the world wide web to expand your knowledge of weather. Keep in mind that web pages change constantly. The web pages below were active at publication date but their continued presence is not guaranteed. But weather-watchers around the world will always be available on the world wide web to teach and advise the budding meteorologist.

Address	Content
sln.fi.edu/weather/index.html	Franklin's Forecast—build your own weather station, learn about today's weather technologies, and check the weather right now. From the Franklin Institute Science Museum.
www.weatherman.com/	Todd Gross' Weather & Astronomy—great weather photos, weather links and tons of weather information.
info.abrfc.noaa.gov/wfodocs/weather_kids.html	Weather for Kids—A great kids weather page as well as many excellent weather links geared toward grades K-8.
windows.ivv.nasa.gov/earth/atmosphere/weather.html	Earth's Weather—a wealth of information about weather and its forces for beginning, intermediate, and advanced learners.
www.nwlink.com/~wxdude/	The "Weather Dude"—Meteorology A to Z, Musical Meteorology, Weather Questions & Quizzes, and much more!